A GALLEON

SERIES EDITOR **R.J. UNSTEAD**

WARWICK PRESS

Series Editor
R. J. Unstead
Author
Jonathan Rutland
Illustrations
John Berry
Michael Trim

Revised edition published 1986 by Warwick Press,
387 Park Avenue South, New York, New York 10016.
First published in 1986 by Kingfisher Books Limited.
Originally published by Hutchinson & Co. Limited 1977.

Library of Congress Catalog Card No. 85-52344
ISBN 0-531-19013-7

CONTENTS

Built for Battle   4
Below Decks   6
Before Sailing   8
Weighing Anchor   11
Masts, Sails, and Rigging   13
Battle at Sea   14
Life at Sea   16
Designing a Galleon   19
Building a Galleon   20
Finding the Way   22
The Story of the *Vasa*   23
Famous Carracks and Galleons   24
Important Happenings   28
Glossary of Terms   29
Index   31

War at Sea

For some 2,000 years, until the battle of Lepanto in 1571, in which a Christian fleet defeated the Turks, war at sea was fought mainly in oared warships called galleys.

From then on, until the arrival of iron and steam in the middle of the 19th century, sea battles were fought in heavily armed sailing ships built specially for battle. These were the galleons, the men-of-war and ships-of-the-line – all of which were very similar in design.

In ancient times sails were used mainly on merchant ships. Warships were rowed. They often carried a mast and sail, but these were lowered before action. These ships were fast and maneuverable, but they were not suitable for long voyages.

During the Middle Ages the rig of sailing ships was improved. A new type of sail became common – the triangular lateen or fore-and-aft sail. With this a ship could sail into the wind and was easier to control. Carracks and caravels with three or four masts and a combination of square and lateen sails were developed. In such vessels the great explorers sailed around Africa to India, and across the Atlantic to the New World.

Long-distance voyaging was soon followed by long-distance sea warfare. To meet this new need shipwrights developed from the ships of Columbus, Drake, and Magellan the sleeker and faster galleon – a ship specially built for warfare.

On the following pages we take a close look at typical galleons of the time. We shall see how they were designed, built, and launched; we shall examine how the crew lived and how they fought battles.

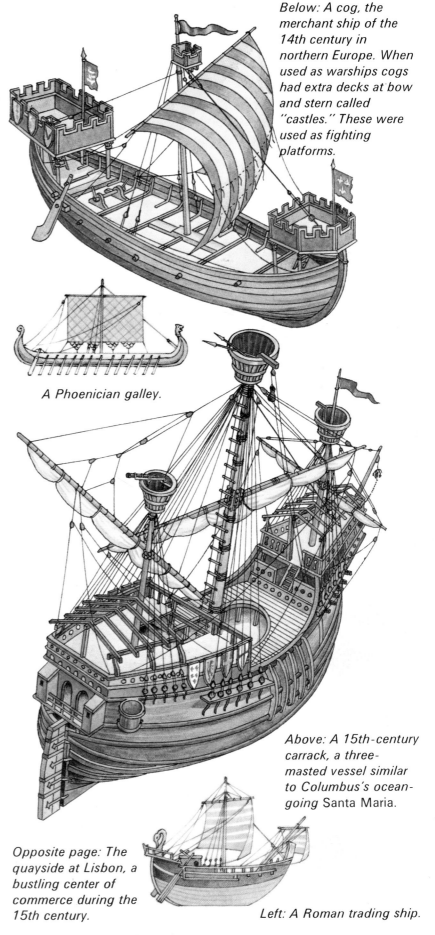

Below: A cog, the merchant ship of the 14th century in northern Europe. When used as warships cogs had extra decks at bow and stern called "castles." These were used as fighting platforms.

A Phoenician galley.

Above: A 15th-century carrack, a three-masted vessel similar to Columbus's ocean-going Santa Maria.

Opposite page: The quayside at Lisbon, a bustling center of commerce during the 15th century.

Left: A Roman trading ship.

3

Built for Battle

The galleon in the picture on the right was built in Holland around the year 1650. Like most men-of-war of that time she has three masts – the mizzen mast (at the stern or back of the ship), the mainmast in the middle, and the foremast at the front.

As you can see, the fore and main masts each have three square sails. The mizzen has a square topsail and a triangular fore-and-aft sail. The two small sails at the bow are the spritsail (under the bowsprit) and the sprit topsail. These helped to make the ship easier to steer. You can read more about sails and rigging on pages 13 and 14.

The galleon's boat is carried in the part of the ship called the waist, on the upper deck. The raised deck near the bow, to the left of the waist, is the forecastle. The raised decks between the main mast and the stern are (from left to right) the half-deck, the quarter-deck, and the poop. On earlier warships these raised decks were much higher. They were platforms from which soldiers could fire down into enemy ships with small "man-killing" guns. But they made the ships top-heavy and difficult to control.

The big "ship-killing" guns developed in the 16th century were too heavy to place high up on the after decks. In galleons they were mounted fairly low in the ship and were fired through gunports, or openings in the side of the ship.

With all sails set, a galleon returns home. The crew have made the anchor at the bow ready for lowering – at sea it is lashed securely so that it cannot swing about and damage the hull. The gunports are all open and the guns run out, ready to fire a salute.

The galleon is around 150 ft (45 m) long, and 40 ft (12 m) wide, and carries over 50 guns (you can see two rows of these in the picture).

The slender beakhead at the bow was probably copied from earlier galleys – in which it was used for ramming. On the galleon the beakhead carried the figurehead, and contained the crew's toilets. The carved and gilded structure built on at the stern is the gallery.

Bowsprit

Main mast

Mizzen-mast

Poop

Quarter-deck

Half-deck

Below Decks

In the large cutaway picture below you can see inside the galleon. A few sailors slept in the forecastle (1), but most lived on the deck below, the gundeck (2). Here, although the cannons took up a lot of space, there was at least plenty of light and air (from the gunports, and from gratings and hatches in the deck above). The officers' "cabins" were in the stern section of this deck (under the captain's cabin – 16). They consisted of canvas screens which were moved before battle.

Often many of the crew had to sleep on the next deck down, the orlop (3). At or below the waterline, with no ports to let in light or air, this deck was dark and smelly. During battle the surgeon worked down here. The anchor cable locker (5), the cookhouse with its brick-lined fire (7), the cannonball store (9) and the sail locker (11) were also all on the orlop deck.

Below this was the hold (12) where barrels of water, beer, salt meat and other provisions were stored, alongside spare sails and ropes. Younger members of the crew were sent here for a punishment known as "holding." The offender was simply lowered into the hold for an hour or two of darkness, dampness and stench. The eerie light of a single lamp was often added to bring out the rats and cockroaches.

The very bottom of the hull, the bilge, was packed with stone ballast (6) which helped to stop the galleon heeling over dangerously. Other parts numbered are the capstans (10) and the bitts, to which the anchor cable was secured (4).

Above: The richly carved and gilded stern of a model of a 17th-century French galleon. Such richly ornamental sterns were merely for show. They were very expensive, and could make the ship top-heavy and unstable.

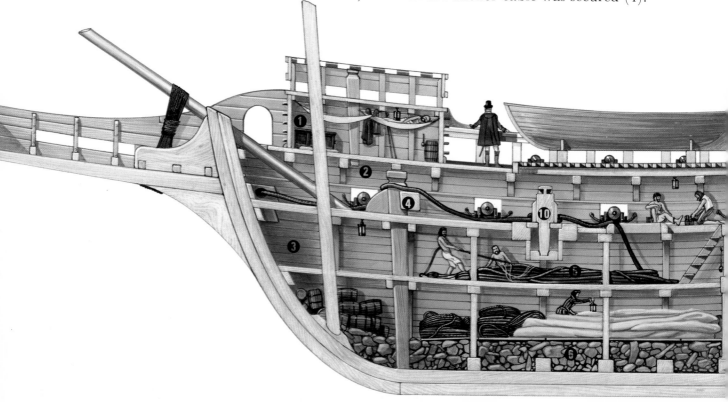

Left: A seaman of 300 years ago — there was no uniform. Most of the food and drink on board was stored in barrels like the one in the picture, so the cooper (the man who made and looked after the barrels) was an important man. Salt beef in a good barrel could be stored for many years — but soon went bad if the barrel was split or holed.

Below: A cutaway view of a two-decker galleon. The two decks referred to are those below the upper deck — the gun deck (2) and the orlop (3).

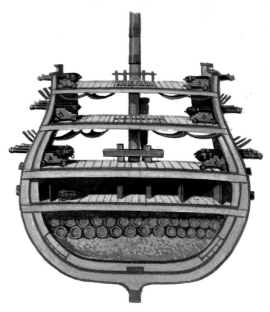

Above: A cross-section of a three-decker. You can see hammocks slung from the ceilings of the gun decks.

The galleon's pump (8) was used to draw any water that might have seeped into the bilges. The capstans (10) were used to haul heavy loads and to raise the anchors.

The rudder (13) controlled the ship's course. It was moved by the tiller (14). Attached to the tiller was a lever called a whipstaff (15) which was operated by the helmsman. Steering wheels were introduced at about the beginning of the 18th century.

Before Sailing

The quayside is busy with activity as food, drink, and equipment arrive for loading. On board seamen check rigging, sails, guns and so on. You can see provisions being taken aboard through hatches in the galleon's side. Heavy items such as guns, or the largest barrels (which weighed nearly half a ton) were lifted by a crane on the quay, or by ropes passing over pulleys on the yard. But once on board there were no cranes to help, and even the half-ton barrels had to be taken down to the hold and stowed by hand. The small cutaway section below shows men stowing provisions in the hold.

Below: In the foreground carpenters are working on the ship's boats, while other members of the crew check and move stores that have just been delivered.

A SEAMAN'S FOOD

The captain took on enough stores for the round trip – which could last several months. These might include around four tons of salt beef and two of salt pork; some salt fish, and perhaps 20,000 ship's biscuits. There would also be dried peas, oatmeal, suet, butter (or oil, which kept better), cheese, and some casks of vinegar. This was used in cooking to hide the taste of stale or bad food. To drink there were around 10,000 gallons of beer, and less than half that amount of water!

Below: In the cutaway part at the stern you can see the admiral discussing the voyage with some of his captains.

Yo-heave-ho

The picture below shows a gang of men turning the capstan to raise the anchor. The anchor cable is far too thick to wind around the capstan. Instead an endless "messenger rope" is used. At the hawsehole where the anchor cable enters the ship it is lashed (or nipped) on to the messenger rope by a length of thin rope called a nipper.

Turning the capstan winds in the messenger rope, which brings the anchor cable with it. As more anchor cable comes in through the hawsehole nippermen lash it to new stretches of the messenger rope. Then they undo the first nippers from the anchor cable which is aboard, and it is passed down and coiled neatly in the hold.

Above: While the anchor is weighed, other members of the crew unfurl the sails.

Below: A fiddler plays a jaunty tune on his violin to help the sailors keep up a steady rhythm at the capstan.

Weighing Anchor

An anchored ship does not float directly above its anchor. If it did, the anchor flukes (the spikes) would not dig into the seabed, and when the ship was lifted by the tide or a wave it would lift the anchor off the bottom.

So when the crew begin to wind in the anchor cable, it is not the anchor that moves but the entire galleon. Shortening the cable pulls the ship through the water until it is above the anchor. Winding the cable in still more lifts the anchor off the seabed — the anchor is "aweigh," and the galleon is free to move.

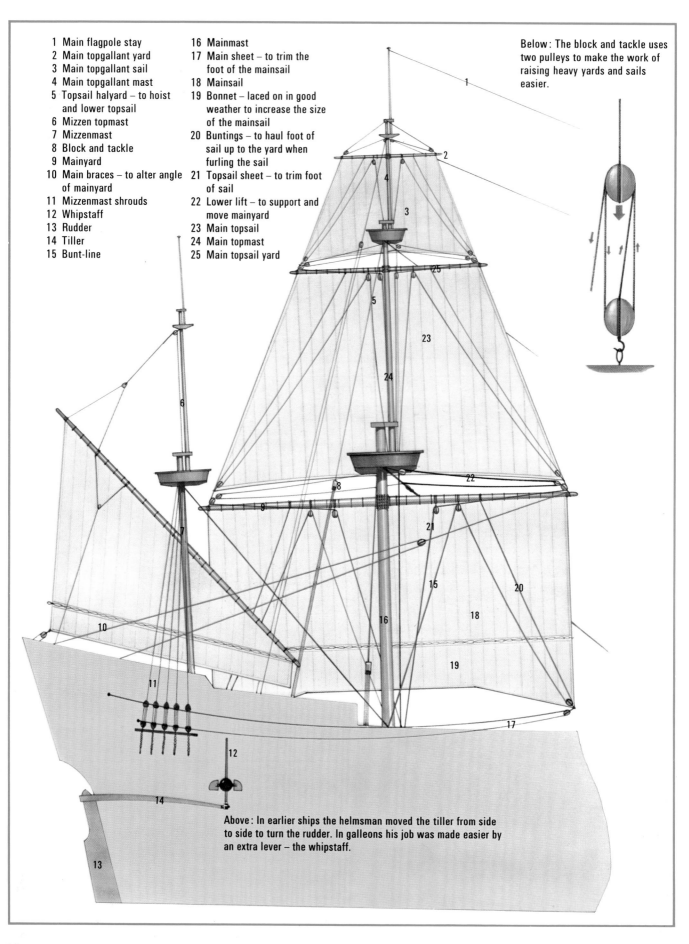

1 Main flagpole stay
2 Main topgallant yard
3 Main topgallant sail
4 Main topgallant mast
5 Topsail halyard – to hoist
  and lower topsail
6 Mizzen topmast
7 Mizzenmast
8 Block and tackle
9 Mainyard
10 Main braces – to alter angle
  of mainyard
11 Mizzenmast shrouds
12 Whipstaff
13 Rudder
14 Tiller
15 Bunt-line

16 Mainmast
17 Main sheet – to trim the
  foot of the mainsail
18 Mainsail
19 Bonnet – laced on in good
  weather to increase the size
  of the mainsail
20 Buntings – to haul foot of
  sail up to the yard when
  furling the sail
21 Topsail sheet – to trim foot
  of sail
22 Lower lift – to support and
  move mainyard
23 Main topsail
24 Main topmast
25 Main topsail yard

Below: The block and tackle uses
two pulleys to make the work of
raising heavy yards and sails
easier.

Above: In earlier ships the helmsman moved the tiller from side
to side to turn the rudder. In galleons his job was made easier by
an extra lever – the whipstaff.

Masts, Sails, and Rigging

The three *masts* are — from bow to stern — the foremast, mainmast, and mizzen. The fore and main masts are both made of three *spars* (poles), called – from bottom to top – the mast, topmast, and topgallant mast. The mizzen has no topgallant mast. The *sails* take their names from their mast: for example, on the foremast they are the foresail, the fore topsail, and the fore

topgallant sail. The *yards* – the poles from which the square sails hang – are named after their sail (main yard, main topsail yard and so on). The sloping spar at the bow is the bowsprit. The small sail at its end is the spritsail topsail, while the sail under the bowsprit is the spritsail.

Above: A galleon sets sail. A gang of seamen unfurl the mainsail, and others in the main top adjust the running rigging.

Below: High winds could tear sails to shreds, so before a storm they had to be "shortened." In the picture the foresail is being furled.

RIGGING

The galleon's sails and spars were supported and controlled by a complicated mass of rigging. The sailors had to know the name and position of every rope. Their safety and the ship's depended on their being able to find the right one without a moment's delay – even in darkness.

There are two main types of rigging – "standing" rigging, which is fixed and supports the masts; and "running" rigging, which is used to raise or trim (adjust) the sails and yards. Standing rigging consists of shrouds, which run from the masthead to the ship's sides, and stays which run from the masthead to another mast or to some other part of the ship. Ratlines tied across each set of shrouds make rope ladders for the seamen to climb. Running rigging consists of "sheets" (for trimming sails), "halyards" (for raising or lowering yards and sails), and "braces" (for setting the angle of a yard).

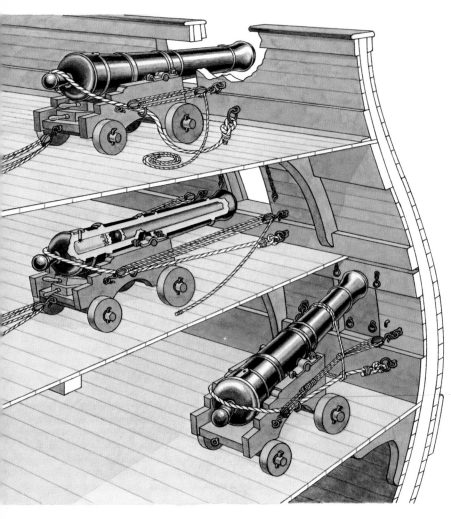

Left: the top gun is shown run out ready for firing, its muzzle sticking out through the open gunport. When the gun is fired the force of the explosion sends the shot forward and pushes the gun back — this is called the recoil. The middle gun is shown in the recoil position — the ropes stop it rolling too far. This gun is cut away to show the touch hole, cartridge, wadding, and shot. These are described on the facing page.

When not in action the gun was firmly tied down. The big guns weighed two or three tons, and if one broke loose it could cause enormous damage.

TACTICS

Opposing fleets usually sailed into battle in parallel lines, so they could fire at each other with "broadsides" from all the guns on one side of each ship. Some cannon were aimed to bring down masts and rigging; others were aimed to put guns out of action.

Battle at Sea

On the command "Clear the decks" men hurry to the gundecks to remove hammocks, bedding, tables and so on. Others climb the rigging to tie the yards extra securely. The boatswain and carpenter prepare their tools and materials, ready to repair any damage which enemy fire inflicts on rigging or hull. The surgeon lays out his instruments, ready to remove splinters (which often caused more damage to the men than the actual shots), to bandage wounds, and to amputate limbs.

The gun crews set out their tools and shot (see the pictures at the top of the next page), together with tubs of water to cool overheated guns. They spread sand and salt on the deck to make it less slippery. They then load their guns, open the gunports and run the guns out ready to fire.

Each gun crew looks after two guns – one on each side of the ship. (One of the captain's greatest fears is to be attacked from both sides at once.) On the command "Fire," the gun captain aims his gun, lights the powder, and stands back.

FIRING THE CANNON

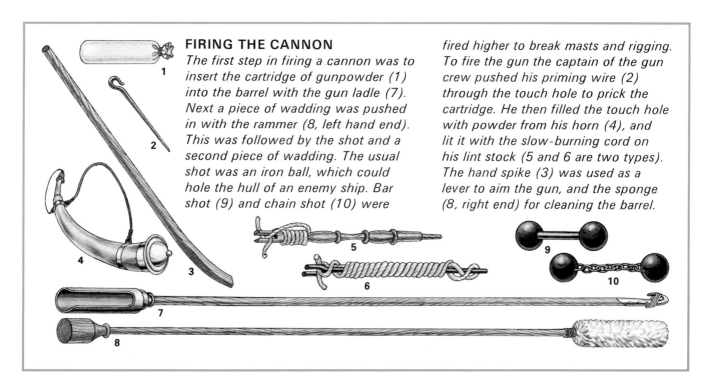

The first step in firing a cannon was to insert the cartridge of gunpowder (1) into the barrel with the gun ladle (7). Next a piece of wadding was pushed in with the rammer (8, left hand end). This was followed by the shot and a second piece of wadding. The usual shot was an iron ball, which could hole the hull of an enemy ship. Bar shot (9) and chain shot (10) were fired higher to break masts and rigging. To fire the gun the captain of the gun crew pushed his priming wire (2) through the touch hole to prick the cartridge. He then filled the touch hole with powder from his horn (4), and lit it with the slow-burning cord on his lint stock (5 and 6 are two types). The hand spike (3) was used as a lever to aim the gun, and the sponge (8, right end) for cleaning the barrel.

Below: The gundeck during battle. Some men are busy at the guns, while others bring more shot. Smoke from the guns is blown back into the ship, and there is little light or air. The scene is crowded, and confused.

Life at Sea

Life on a galleon was hard and uncomfortable. The crew slept and ate on the gundecks. Gunports and hatches could be opened to let in light and air only in fine weather, so conditions were often dark, airless, smelly – and wet. The galleon's timbers "worked" (moved), and in rough seas seams opened, letting in gushes of water.

Rats, cockroaches, and other bugs were common. The food was often rancid, too hard to chew, or full of weevils. The beer was sour; fresh fruit and vegetables were rare. During a long voyage far more seamen died of illness than in battle.

Pigs, goats, chickens or other animals were kept in pens on the galleon to provide fresh meat, eggs, butter, and cheese – mostly for the captain, and officers' tables. Sometimes the captain had his own cook, and a special oven in which food could be baked or roasted.

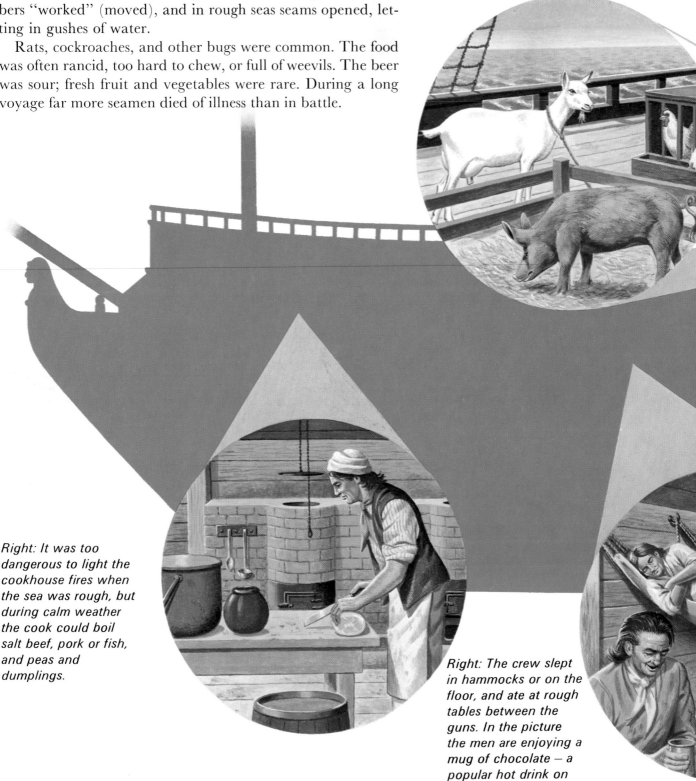

Right: It was too dangerous to light the cookhouse fires when the sea was rough, but during calm weather the cook could boil salt beef, pork or fish, and peas and dumplings.

Right: The crew slept in hammocks or on the floor, and ate at rough tables between the guns. In the picture the men are enjoying a mug of chocolate – a popular hot drink on board.

JOBS AT SEA

In rough seas a sailor's work was difficult and dangerous. He had to climb up in the rigging to take in sails, or to fit new ones – a high wind could tear the canvas or break masts.

In fair weather the crew was kept busy swabbing the decks, trimming sails, cleaning the guns, and doing repairs.

Above: Sewing up any rips in the canvas sails, and checking the ropes for wear were just two of the many repair jobs which kept sailors busy at sea.

Top: The captain lived in much greater comfort than his crew. He had a spacious cabin in the aftercastle with large windows. His food store included luxuries such as dried fruit, bacon, sugar, and wine.

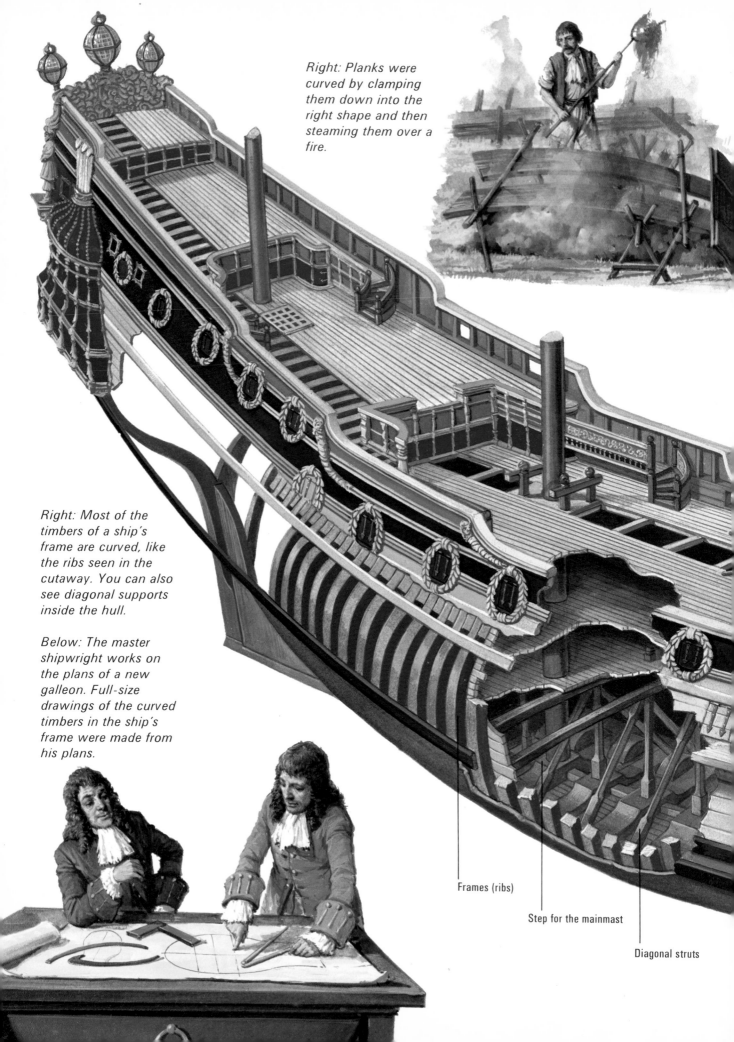

Right: Planks were curved by clamping them down into the right shape and then steaming them over a fire.

Right: Most of the timbers of a ship's frame are curved, like the ribs seen in the cutaway. You can also see diagonal supports inside the hull.

Below: The master shipwright works on the plans of a new galleon. Full-size drawings of the curved timbers in the ship's frame were made from his plans.

Frames (ribs)

Step for the mainmast

Diagonal struts

Designing a Galleon

Early shipwrights designed vessels mainly by eye. They watched any ships visiting their home port, compared their shapes, and saw how well they sailed. They developed an eye for a seaworthy vessel, and when building a ship they followed a picture in their mind's eye.

But it was not possible to build a large, complicated galleon in this way. By the late 1550s shipwrights usually drew detailed plans for the shipyard. From about 1650 they often made a scale model as well, like the one shown here.

Galleons were made of oak, a very strong and hard wood, and a single ship needed around 2,000 trees. Its length was usually three or four times its greatest width. The underwater lines were based on fish shapes — rounded at the bow and narrowing down to a slim, streamlined stern.

Above: Shipbuilders went to the forests armed with molds of the ship's parts. They searched for trees to match the shapes.

Below: The amount of gold decoration on a galleon in the 1600s is clearly seen in the horseman on the beakhead. The wreaths around the gunports are also gilded.

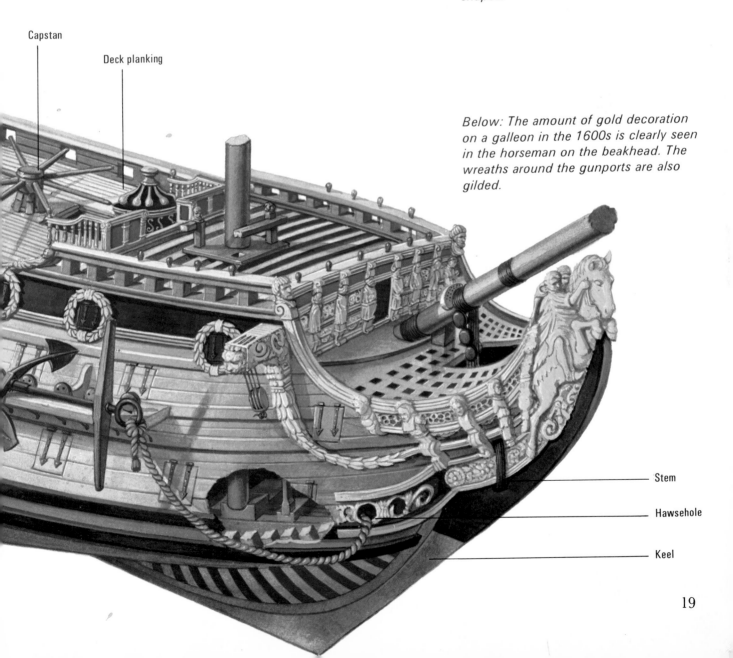

Capstan

Deck planking

Stem

Hawsehole

Keel

Building a Galleon

The first step was to lay the keel – the backbone on which the rest of the frame was built up. As this was often 100 feet (30 meters) or more long, it was made of several lengths of timber jointed and bolted together. The stempost and sternpost – which formed the bow and stern – were then jointed and bolted to the keel. The joint between sternpost and keel was strengthened with a massive timber "knee," held in place with long bolts.

The V-shaped ground timbers on which the ribs would be built up were now bolted to the keel. To hold them firmly in place a keelson was added. This was an upper keel which slotted over the middle of each V piece and was bolted to the keel – thus clamping the ground timbers between keel and keelson. Next the ribs were built up on their ground timbers. Like the keel they were too large to be shaped from a single log, and were made of several pieces joined together. You can see the basic skeleton of keel, sternpost, stempost and ribs in the picture above.

Left: Sawing planks. Below: The carpenter's tools.

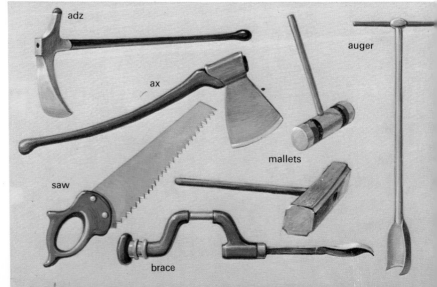

adz

auger

ax

mallets

saw

brace

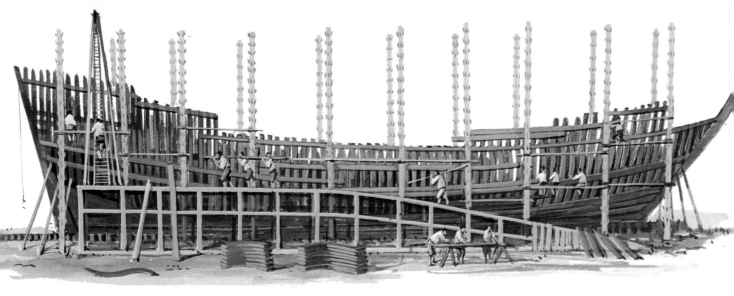

Above: On the level of each deck, beams were fixed across the ship from the rib on one side to its partner on the other. The joint between rib and beam was strengthened with "knees" (you can see piles of these on the ground in the picture).

The strength of the ship depended on its skeleton, so all joints had to be really firm – and all the timbers massive *(they were often over 1½ ft – ½ meter – square). Once the skeleton was complete, planking could begin. The planks, up to 5 in (13 cm) thick, were laid edge to edge, and were held in place with wooden pegs called treenails – iron nails would soon rust away. The hull then had to be made watertight by caulking before it was ready for launching.*

Above: Caulking or waterproofing was done by forcing yarn or tar between the planks of the hull. After this, the underwater planks might be coated with tar and hair. To launch the galleon (below), workmen first built a "cradle" under the keel, and fixed supports between the hull and cradle to hold the ship upright (you can see these supports near bow and stern in the picture). Next the scaffolding, the supporting poles, and the blocks on which the keel had been laid (and which had taken the vessel's weight until now) were removed. Finally gangs of men on shore and at capstans on barges in the water hauled and pushed the cradle and its load down into the water. The cradle slid along a shallow trough well greased with tallow (animal fat). Masts, spars, and so on were added when the hull was afloat.*

Finding the Way

Francis Drake sailed his galleon *Golden Hind* around the world, and many other captains made long voyages across uncharted oceans. They found their way partly by guesswork, partly by following steady "trade winds", and partly by using the sun and stars.

On setting sail from port the captain knew his direction from his compass, and could estimate his speed. So after a few hours (timed with a sand glass) he could mark his new position on a chart. This was called "dead reckoning". It depended on the captain's skill in estimating how far the wind and current had taken him off course.

The log line helped to measure speed. A length of cord was knotted at equal spaces, and a piece of wood fixed to one end was dropped overboard. The number of knots slipping through a seaman's fingers in one minute gave the approximate speed in "knots" (nautical miles an hour).

On the equator the sun is overhead at noon. The farther north or south one travels, the lower the sun is in the sky. So by measuring the sun's altitude at noon (its height above the horizon), sailors could work out their distance north or south of the equator (latitude).

Above: An early mariner's compass. The card and its magnetized needle pivoted on a pin.

Above: Using a backstaff to measure the sun's height above the horizon.

Below: Speed was checked by sand glass (left) and log line.

Below: A map of the world drawn in 1570. Maps and charts helped the captain plot his course across the open seas.

22

THE STORY OF THE VASA

One Sunday morning in 1628 the people of Stockholm in Sweden gathered to watch the galleon *Vasa* set sail on her maiden voyage. She was the largest, most richly gilded, and most powerfully armed ship in the Swedish navy.

She sailed smoothly out for perhaps 10 minutes, when a sudden squall of wind heeled her over. Water poured in through the open gunports in the lower gun deck, and within minutes only the tip of the mainmast remained above water.

The next day a court of inquiry opened to find who was responsible for the disaster. The king of Sweden himself had approved *Vasa*'s design, so the shipwrights could hardly be blamed.

Had the gunnery officer secured the guns properly? Yes, he had.

Had the sailing master stowed the ballast correctly? Yes, he had. In his opinion the ship was top-heavy – too much weight high above the water.

Perhaps *Vasa* was just unlucky. Sudden squalls are always dangerous to sailing ships, and with the excitement on board, and a new crew, the disaster could have been the result of carelessness.

Attempts to salvage *Vasa* began at once. Divers recovered most of the guns – but they could not budge the actual ship. In 1956 Anders Franzen rediscovered the wreck, lying buried in mud at the bottom of Stockholm harbor. The hull was raised in 1961.

Above: This drawing of the Vasa is based on reconstruction suggestions.

23

FAMOUS CARRACKS AND GALLEONS

Henry VIII's *Henry Grâce à Dieu* (right) or the *Great Harry* (1514) was the super ship of her day, being a four-masted carrack of 1,000 tons over 165 ft (50 m) long and originally with 186 guns, some of them able to fire a 60 pounder (27 kg) ball. However, her narrow beam, towering poop and big forecastle made her liable to list or even to capsize, so that it was probably fortunate that she never took part in a sea battle. The *Great Harry* may well have been built to answer the challenge of the *Great Michael*, an impressive "great ship" built by a Frenchman for James IV of Scotland.

The *São João* (1534) was a four-masted warship whose appearance is known from a tapestry now in Madrid. A galleon, built to supersede the carrack or great ship, she was a more efficient fighting ship than any contemporary vessel belonging to Spain.

Against the Spanish Armada, Martin Frobisher commanded the

Henry Grâce à Dieu or "Great Harry"

Triumph (1561), a royal galleon of 1,100 tons, which made her the biggest ship on either side. Contrary to popular legend, the real fighting ships of the Spanish and English fleets were pretty well equal to one another in size. The Spanish guns could fire heavier shot, but the

English had the advantage at long range, which helps to explain Lord Howard's tactics in the English Channel.

The *Revenge* (1577), Drake's flagship, when he was second-in-command to Lord Howard, considered to be the finest warship of its time. Of only 500 tons, it was "low and snug in the water," highly maneuverable and armed with a broadside of 34 guns, ranging from 9–32 pounders 4–15 kg. Her end came in 1591 off the Azores, after her commander, Sir Richard Grenville and his crew fought a Spanish fleet of 53 ships all one day and night.

Howard of Effingham's flagship, The *Ark Royal* 800 tons, which the Queen had bought from Sir Walter Raleigh, was similar to the *Revenge* in design, armament and crew, who numbered about 250.

The *Girona* sailed with the Spanish Armada to invade England in 1588. The English chased the defeated Spanish galleons as far as the Firth

Treasures from the Girona

of Forth, but then gave up the chase as they had no gunpowder left. In 1967 Robert Stenuit, a Belgian archaeologist discovered gold treasures (bottom left) when diving in the vicinity of the sunken Girona.

The *Golden Hind* (below) in which Drake circumnavigated the world in 1577–80, weighed 100 tons was only about 98 ft (30 m) long and 23 ft (7 m) wide, but she could outsail most other ships.

Built by Phineas Pett for James I in 1610, the *Prince Royal* 1,200 tons was the largest ship afloat and is often said to have been the first English three-decker, with 56 guns (later 90) on three levels, although one was merely an armed upper deck. A more remarkable feature was the lavish carving, gilding and painting of her upper works.

For Charles I, Pett built the even larger *Sovereign of the Seas* (1637), a real three-decker of 1,500 tons and 100 guns; she carried a greater spread of sail than any previous warship, including "royals" on fore and mainmast and a topgallant sail on mizzen. Renamed *Royal Sovereign* by Charles II, she was accidentally destroyed by fire in 1696.

During the 1630's, Cardinal Richelieu, Louis XIII's minister of state, created a French navy of nearly 40 excellent warships, including one to compare with the great *Sovereign of the Seas*. This was the *Couronne* (1638), a two-decker about 249 ft (76 m) in length and carrying 72 guns and a crew of 600 men. The French preferred a ship with a wider beam, shallower draft and lower deckline than the English man-of-war, believing that their ship would be a better gun platform and a more efficient sailer.

Overleaf: The defeat of the Spanish Armada in 1588. In the foreground is a galleass, a cross between a galley and a galleon. The battle was mainly between the sleek English galleons and the Spanish "floating fortresses."

The Golden Hind

IMPORTANT HAPPENINGS

1487

1487–8 Bartolomeo Diaz sails from Lisbon around the tip of South Africa (Cape of Good Hope).

1497–8 Vasco da Gama sails from Lisbon to India with a fleet of four ships.

1497(?)1504 Amerigo Vespucci makes four voyages to South America, two in the service of Spain, two for Portugal.

1492 Christopher Columbus reaches the West Indies in 69 days aboard the *Santa Maria*, a three-masted carrack of about 100 tons. Two tiny caravels, the *Pinto* 50 tons and *Niña* 40 tons, accompany him.

1500 About this time the first large "ship-killing" guns are used on warships. Gunports are added to the ship's sides, so that the big guns can be carried lower down in the hull – where they are less likely to make the ship top heavy.

1500s The after castle begins to become wider in construction in the caravel and later in the galleon. The galleon begins to adopt its developed form: square, low forecastle, long beak, and longer hull. The primitive tiller is replaced by the whipstaff.

1519 Ferdinand Magellan sets out with five ships to discover a western route to the Spice Islands. He sails through Magellan Strait and across the Pacific Ocean to the Philippines where he is killed. One ship, the *Vittoria,* returns to Spain, with only 18 crew alive, the first men to circumnavigate the world.

1550

1571 The battle of Lepanto (see below). Don John of Austria, commanding a fleet of over 200 galleys and galleasses, defeats the Ottoman navy in the Gulf of Corinth, thereby destroying Turkish sea-power.

1577–80 Francis Drake sails around the world in his galleon *The Pelican* which he renames the *Golden Hind.*

1588 The Spanish Armada of some 130 vessels includes a few galleasses, but the battle is mainly between lower-built and more maneuverable English galleons and the Spanish "floating fortresses." The nimble English ships shadow the enemy, but their long-range gunnery does little serious damage.

1600 The galleon is at its most developed in the early 1600s. Many are three-deckers, carrying between 70 and 100 guns. Galleons now have a square mizzen sail and a spritsail topmast at the end of the bowsprit.

1600s Sea battles between French, Dutch, Spanish, and British vessels lead to construction of bigger warships. Changes in sails follow, and the towering upper-works of the galleon become more streamlined.

1700s Britain's lead in warship construction is challenged by the French and Dutch. The whipstaff is replaced by a wheel which swings the rudder through ropes and pulleys.

1805

1805 The battle of Trafalgar. British navy under Horatio Nelson defeats a combined French and Spanish fleet off southern Spain. Warships of 2,000 tons, with 100 guns on three decks, fight at close quarters, firing terrible broadsides before boarding parties board the enemy ships.

GLOSSARY OF TERMS

Abaft Behind, toward the stern.

Abeam Across the ship, at right angles to its length.

Aft At or near the stern of a ship.

Ahead Directly in front of the bows.

Amidships In the middle of a ship.

Anchor Heavy piece of iron which digs into the sea bed to hold a ship to the spot.

Astern Backward — behind the stern.

Athwartships Across the ship, from one side to the other.

Awash Level with the surface of the sea.

Ballast Heavy material such as stones in the bottom of the hold to help keep the ship upright.

Beak A strong projection of the prow (or bow) which smashed oncoming waves when a ship pitched or dipped low in a rough sea.

Beam Width of ship at its widest point.

Berth Place where a ship ties up.

Bilge The bottom of a ship.

Bonaventure An extra mizzen mast on a four-mast ship.

Boom A pole along the foot of a sail.

Bow The sharp front end of a ship.

Bowsprit A long spar at the bow.

Bridge Raised deck from which a ship is navigated.

Broadside Shots from all the guns on one side of a ship.

Bulkhead Wall dividing up the inside of a ship.

Buoy A floating marker moored in the water to guide or warn ships.

Buoyancy The ability of an object to float.

Capstan A revolving windlass or drum-shaped device for winding in anchor cable.

Carvel-built (Of a wooden ship): having its planks laid edge to edge.

Caulking Making seams between planks watertight with pitch (tar).

Chart Map of the sea and coastal waters.

Clinker-built (Of a wooden ship): having its planks overlapping.

Deck Nautical word for floor.

Dock The working area of a harbor where ships are loaded, unloaded and repaired.

Draft Depth of a ship below the water.

Fathom Unit of length used for measuring the depth of water, equal to 6 ft (1.83 m).

Following wind One blowing from astern (behind).

Forecastle, or Fo'c'sle Raised deck in the bows. Often used to describe accommodation in the bows for the crew.

Forward Near the front or bow.

Freeboard Height from waterline to the top of the hull.

Galley A ship's kitchen.

Gear Nautical word for machinery or equipment — e.g. steering gear, ship's gear (derricks, cranes etc. for loading cargo).

Gunwale (gunnel) Upper edge of a ship's or boat's side.

Hatch An opening in a deck, or its wooden cover.

Heel When a sailing ship is blown over to one side it is said to heel over.

Helm Steering control of a ship.

Hogging The tendency of a ship to droop at bow and stern when it rides over a wave.

Hold The lowest part of the hull, where cargo is stored.

Hull The body of a ship.

Keel The main timber at the bottom of a ship (the spine).

Knot A speed of a nautical mile an hour.

Lateen A triangular sail which is set along the ship ('fore-and-aft'), not across it.

Latitude Distance north or south of the equator, measured in degrees, from 0° on the equator to 90° at the poles.

Leeward Direction toward which the wind blows. The lee side of a ship is therefore the sheltered side, away from the wind.

Longitude Distance east or west of the Greenwich zero meridian, measured in degrees east or west of Greenwich.

Mizzen Fore-and-aft sail on aftermost mast of a three-mast ship; also the mizzen may refer to the mast itself.

Right: An illustration from a book printed in 1585 shows fire bombs and cannon balls headed for a Swedish ship. Other kinds of shot commonly used were explosive bombs (hollow iron balls filled with gunpowder); hot shot (solid balls which were heated before being placed in the gun) and chain shot (two iron balls linked by a chain).

Moor To secure a ship, either against a quay, or by tying it to a mooring buoy, or by dropping anchor.

Nautical mile A distance of 6,076.1 ft (1,852 m).

Orlop A deck beneath the lower gundeck and above the hold.

Pitching The plunging and rising movements of a ship as it rides across the waves.

Poop The aftercastle: a raised deck at the stern.

Port The left-hand side of a ship, looking forward.

Porthole An opening in the side of a ship to let in light and air and for cannon to fire through.

Quarterdeck Part of upper-deck between stern and mizzenmast.

Rake The slope of masts, funnels, bows, etc.

Ratlines Ropes knotted across the shrouds to provide a rope ladder to the masthead.

Rigging The ropes used to support masts, and to control sails and spars.

Rudder Large, flat wooden blade at the stern, used to turn a ship.

Sheet Rope used for setting and trimming a sail.

Shroud Rope from masthead to ship's side, supporting mast.

Spar Wooden pole such as mast or yard.

Spritsail A small square sail fitted to the bowsprit.

Square sail A sail set across the ship, from side to side.

Starboard Right hand side of ship.

Stay Rope which helps support a mast.

Stempost The curved timber at the bow to which a ship's sides are joined.

Stern The back of the ship.

Superstructure Upper parts of a ship, built on top of the hull.

Tiller Length of wood fitted to the top of the rudder, for steering.

Trim To adjust the balance of a ship or boat; to move yards or sails to suit wind. Also the way a ship floats in the water.

Wake or Wash The waves and foam caused by a moving ship.

Watch A spell of duty for a seaman.

Windward Direction from which the wind blows. The windward side is therefore the one exposed to the wind.

Yard A spar (or pole) slung across a mast to support a sail.

INDEX

A
anchor 4, 6, 7, 10, 11
animals 16
Ark Royal 24
Armada, Spanish 3

B
backstaff 22
ballast 6, 23
barrels 6, 7, 8
battle 14, 15
beakhead 4, 19
bilge 7
bitts 6, 7
broadsides 14, 18

C
cannonball 6
cannons 6
capstan 6, 7, 10, 19
captain 7, 9, 16, 17
caravel 3
carpenters 8, 14
  tools 20
carrack 3
castles 3, 4, 5, 6
  aftercastle 17
  forecastle 4, 6
caulking 21
cog 3
Columbus, Christopher 3
compass 22
cookhouse 6, 16
Couronne 25

D
dead reckoning 22
decks 4, 6, 7, 17, 23
Drake, Sir Francis 3, 22, 24–25

F
Franzen, Anders 23

G
galleass 23

Girona 25
Golden Hind 22, 23, 25
Great Harry 24
gun deck 6, 7, 14, 15, 23
gunports 4, 6, 14, 16, 19, 23
gunpowder 15
guns 4, 8, 14, 15, 17, 23

H
hammocks 7, 14, 16
hatches 6, 8, 10, 16
hawsehole 10, 19
helmsman 7
Henry VIII 24
hold 6, 8, 10
hull 6, 14, 21, 23

J
John, Don, of Austria 23

K
keel 19, 20, 21
knots 22

L
launching 21
Lepanto, battle of 3, 23
loading 8, 9
log line 22

M
Magellan, Ferdinand 3
maps 22
masts 3, 4, 12, 13, 14, 17, 23

N
navigation 22
nipper 10

O
officers 6, 7, 16
  cabins 6, 7
orlop 6, 7

P
Phoenician galley 3

Prince Royal 25
provisions 6, 7, 8, 9, 16
pumps 6, 17
punishments 6

Q
quayside 8, 9

R
race-built galleon 4, 5, 23
Revenge 24
rigging 12, 13, 14, 17
Roman trading ship 3

S
sails 3, 4, 8, 12, 13, 17, 23
  furling 13
  repairing 17
  unfurling 10
Salamis, battle of 3
sand glass 22
Santa Maria 3, 23
São João 24
seamen 7
shanties 10
ship building 20, 21
ship designing 18, 19
shipwright 18, 19
shot 14, 15
Sovereign of the Seas 25
stern 4, 6, 19, 20, 21
surgeon 6, 14

T
tactics 14
timbers 9, 16, 18, 19, 20
tools 14, 15
trade wind 22
Triumph 24

V
Vasa 23

Y
yards 10, 12, 13, 14

PHOTOGRAPHIC ACKNOWLEDGEMENTS
The publishers wish to thank the following for supplying photographs for this book: Page 2 Giraudon; 22 Science Museum, London *top*; Michael Holford *bottom*; 23 Vasa Museum, Sweden; Tourist Section Swedish Embassy *bottom*; 24 Mansell *top*; Ulster Museum Belfast *bottom*; 25 Mansell; 26–27 Michael Holford; 28 National Maritime Museum.

Picture research: Jackie Cookson